All images were developed with lots of love and care,
so you can have a lot of fun.
Happy painting!

Jesus loves you

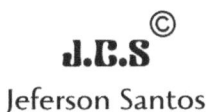

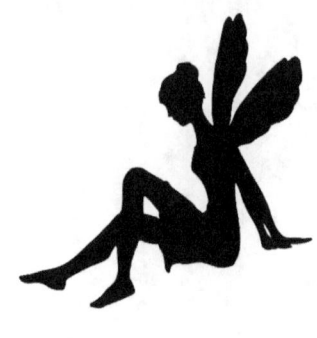

This Book Belongs to:

_____

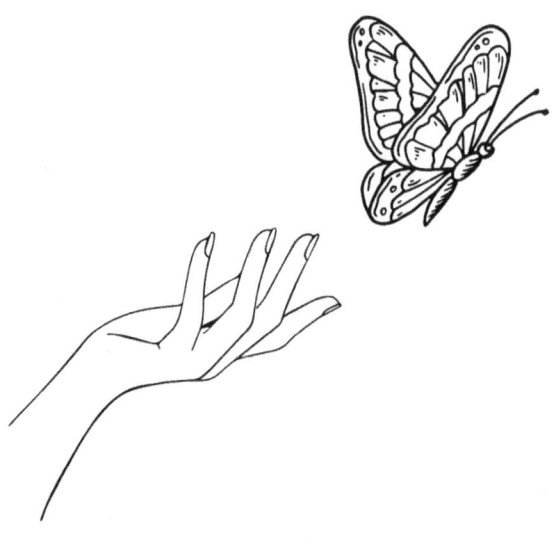

ALL RIGHTS RESERVED
2024

No part of this publication may be reproduced, distributed, or transmitted in any form or by any means, including photocopying, recording, or other electronic or mechanical methods, without the prior written permission of the publisher, except for brief quotations incorporated in critical reviews and other specific noncommercial uses. Any unauthorized replica of this work is prohibited.

J.C.S©

Jeferson Santos

Test Color Page

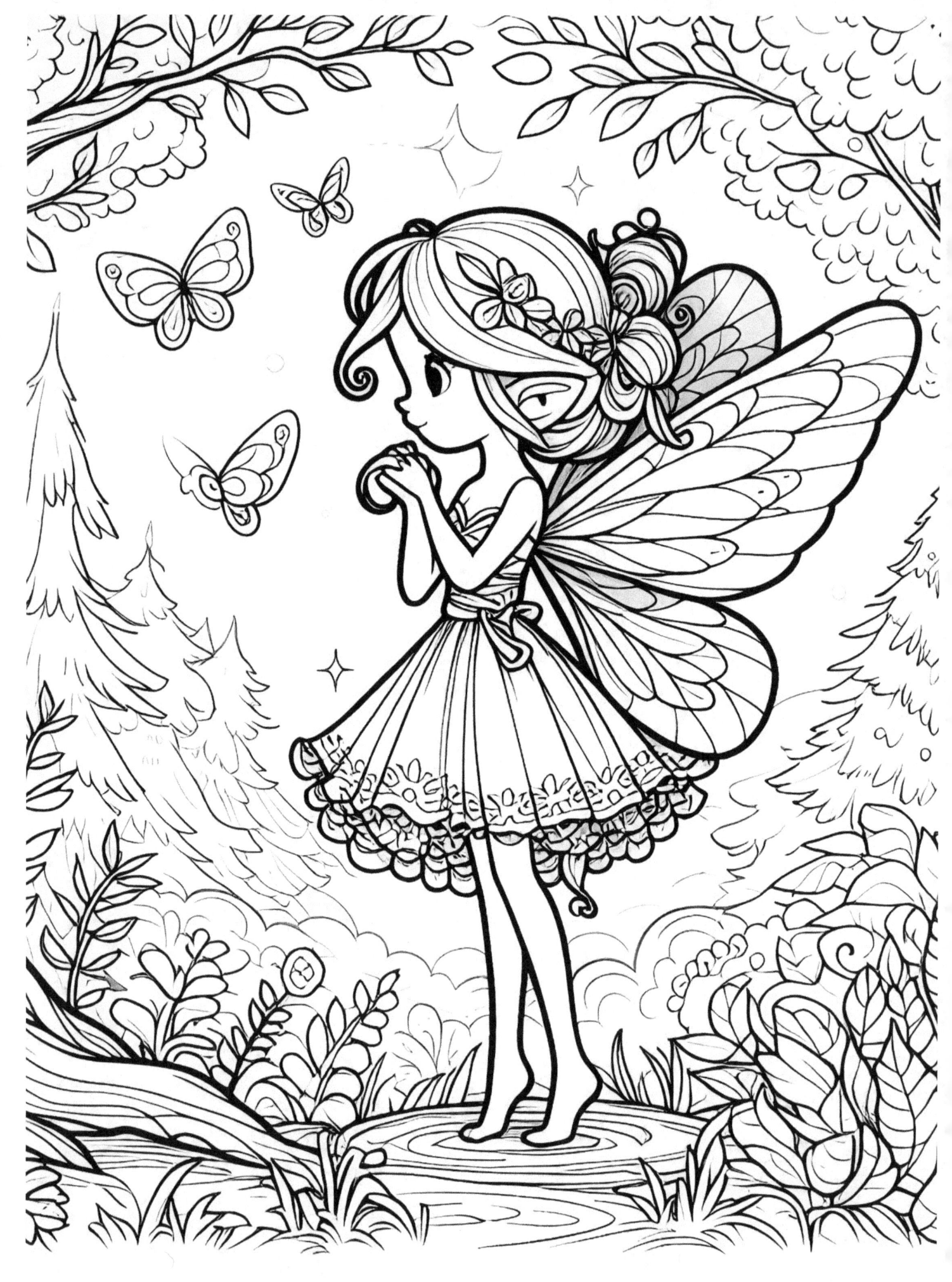

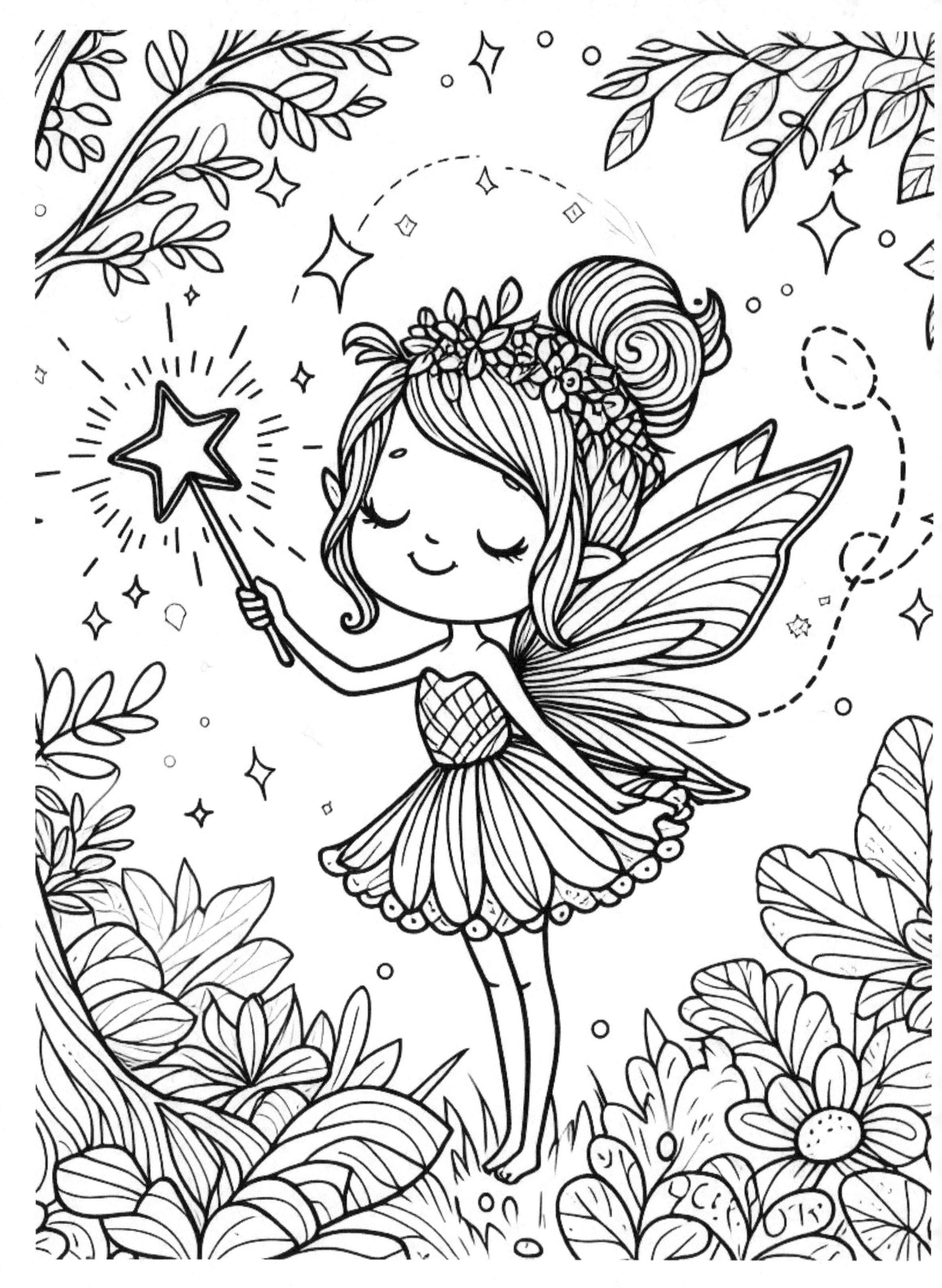

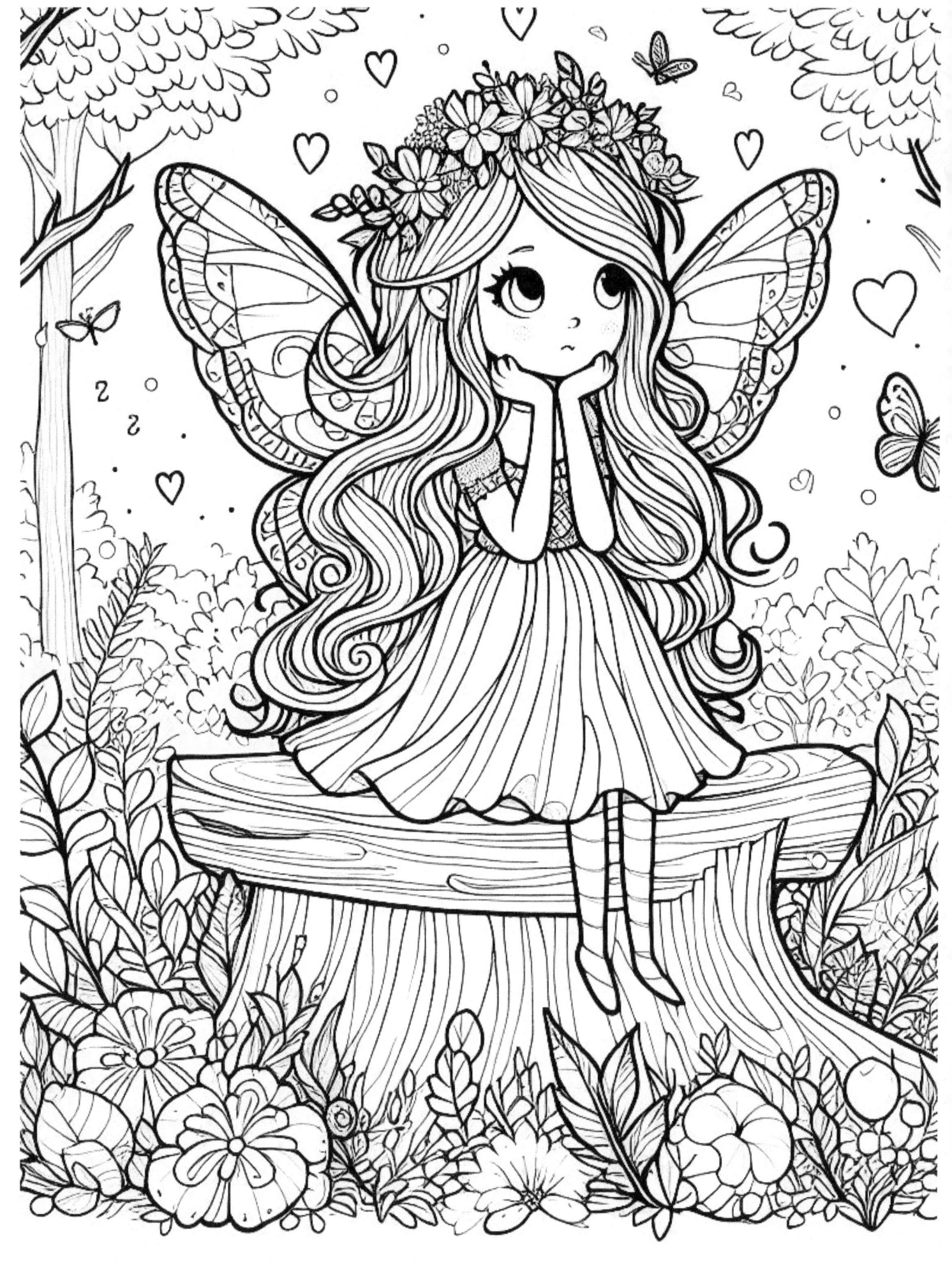

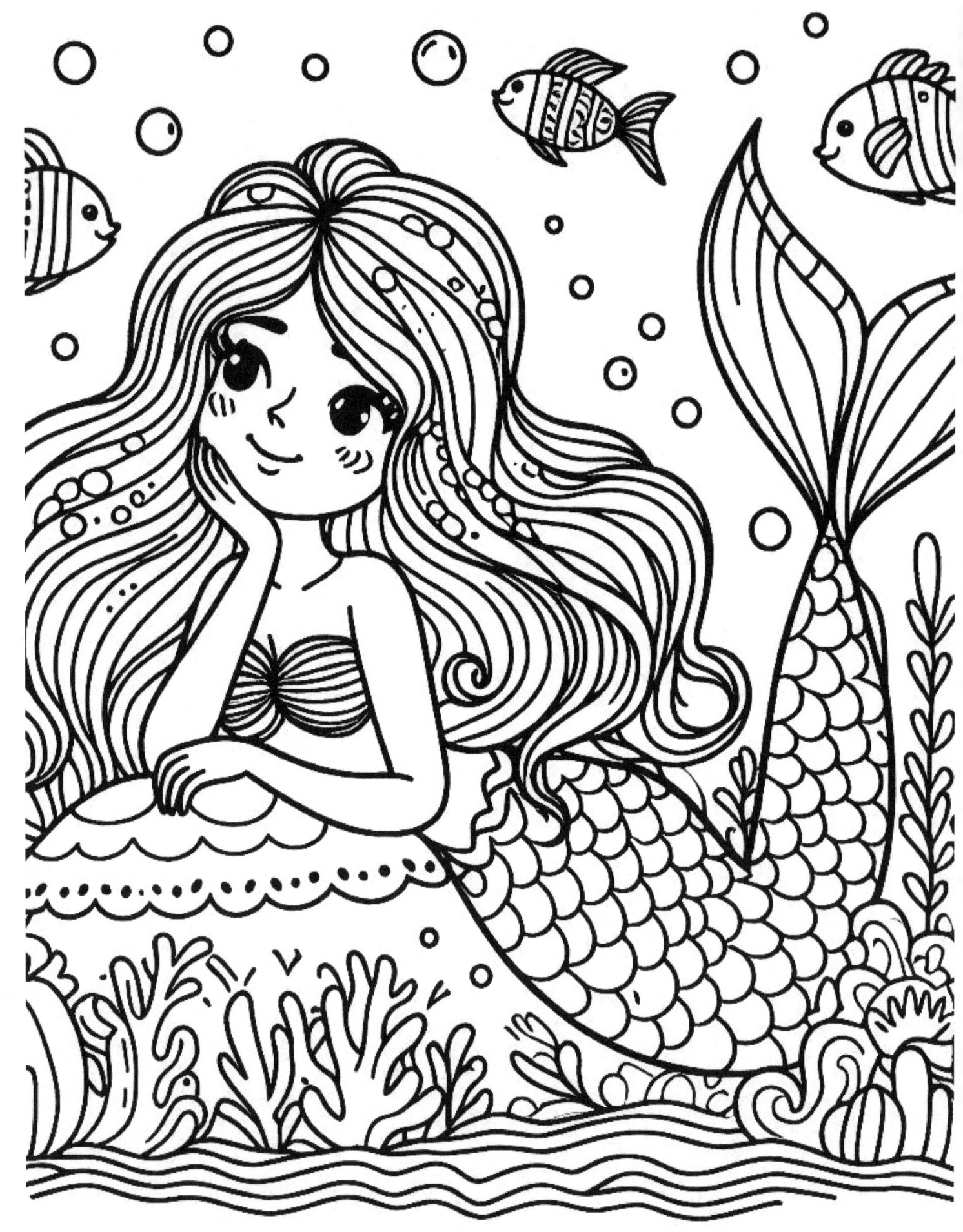

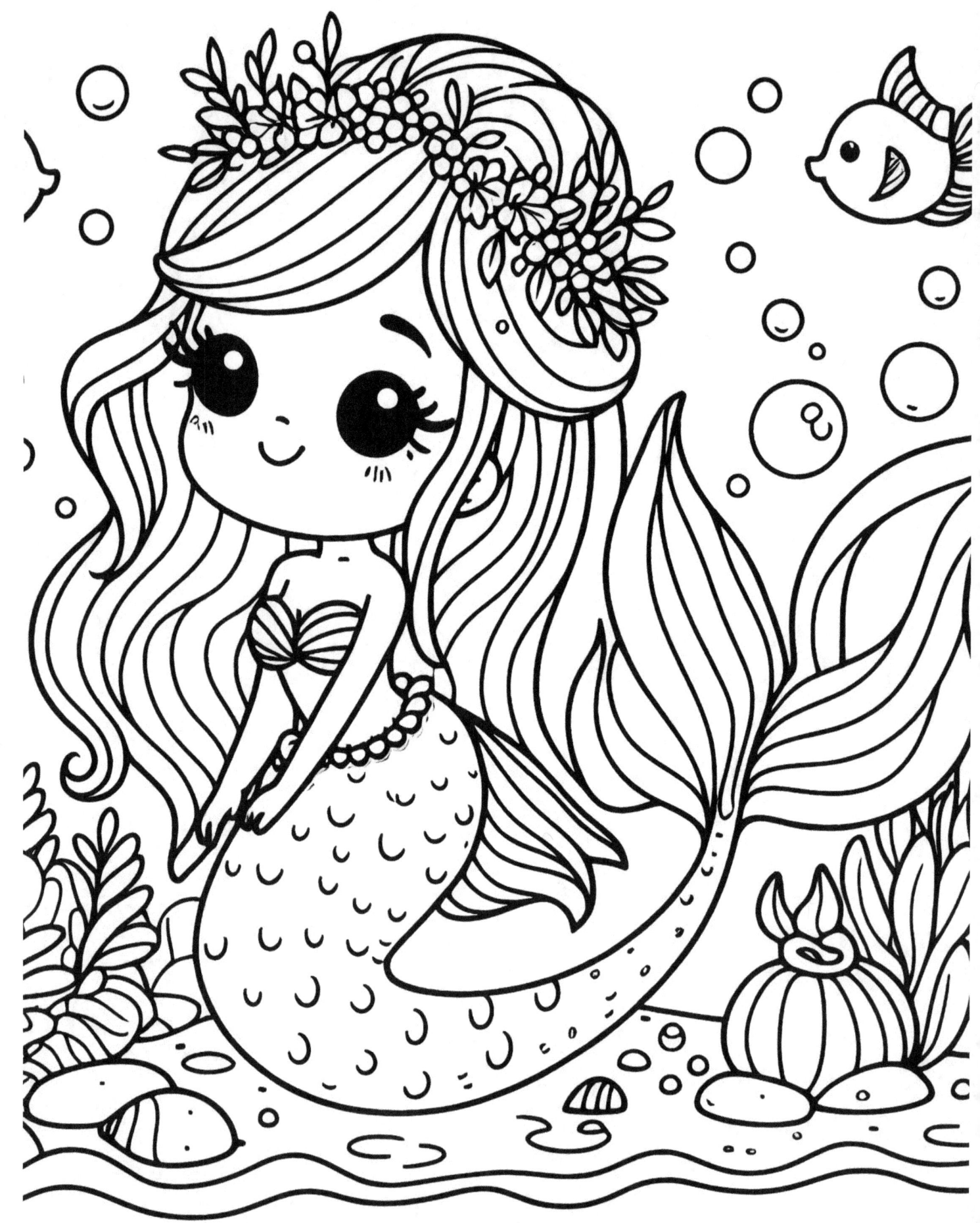

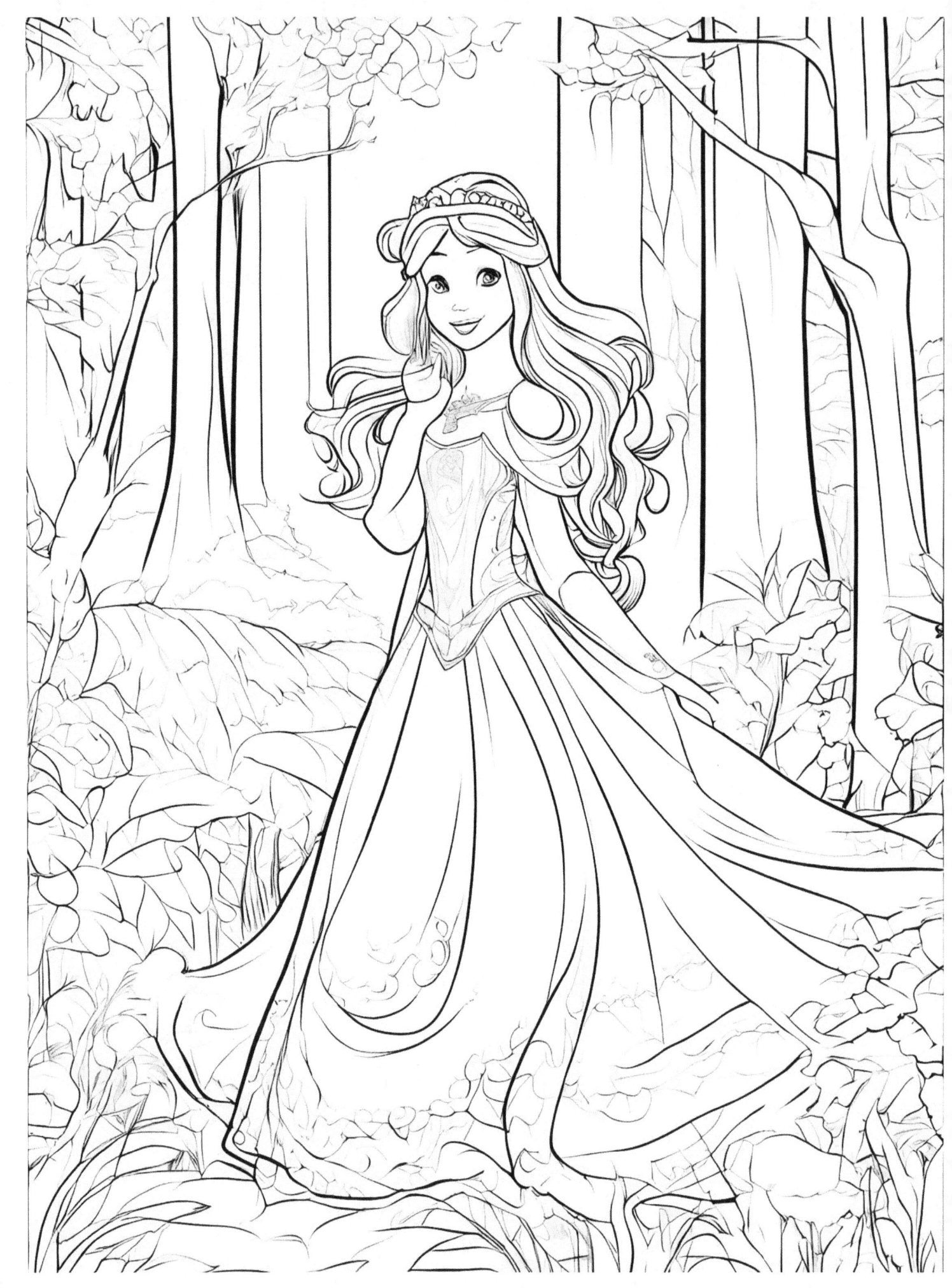

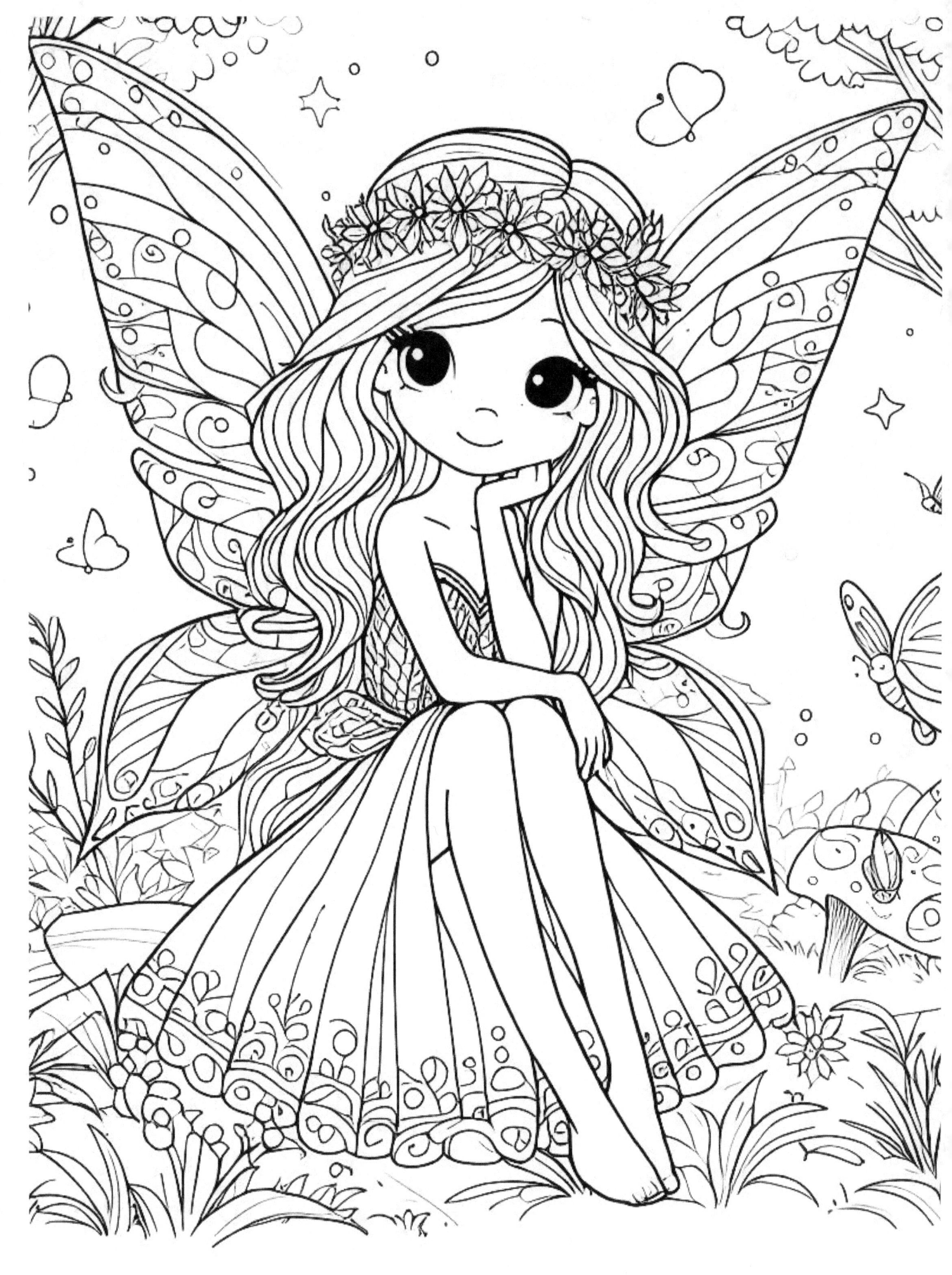

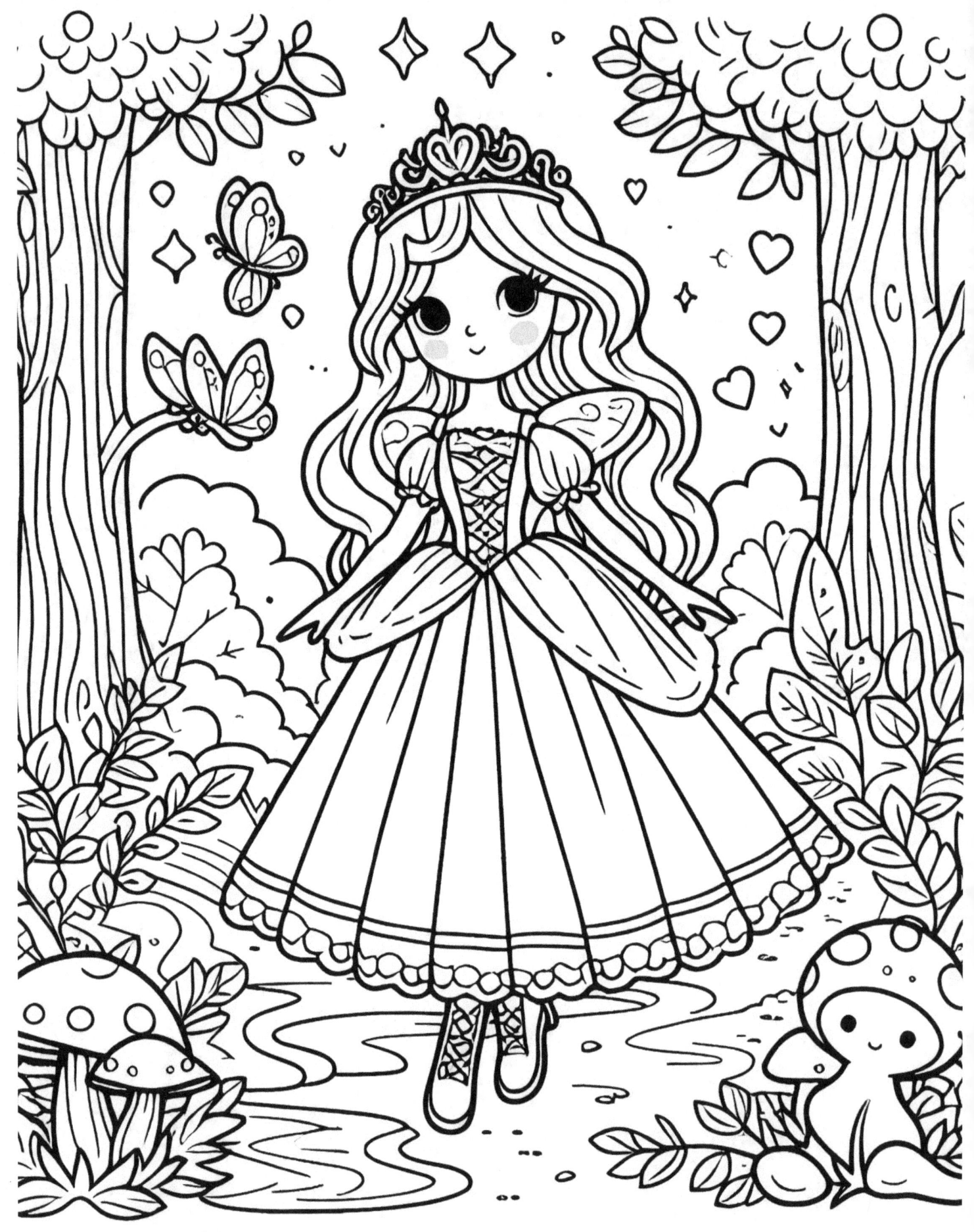

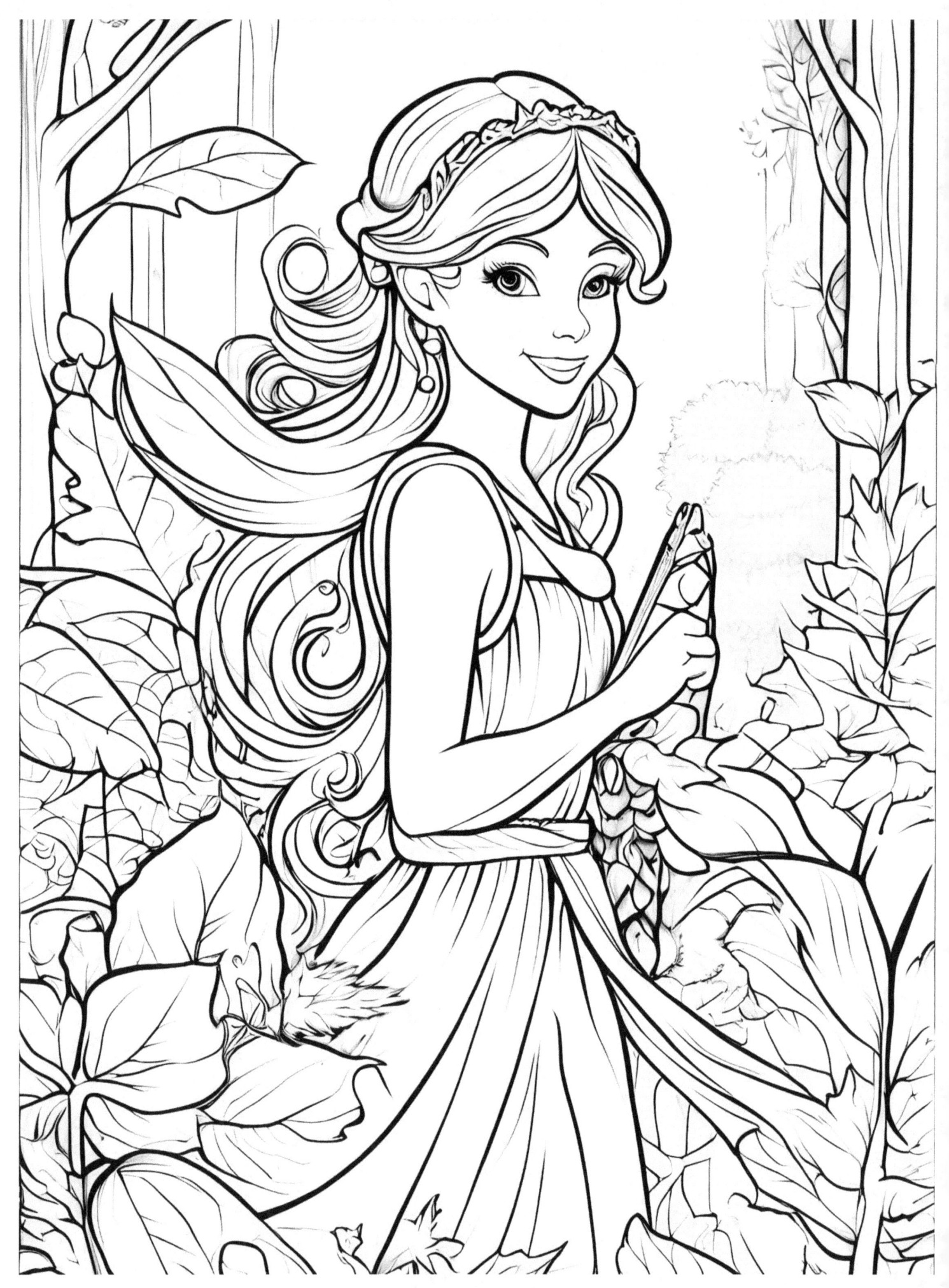

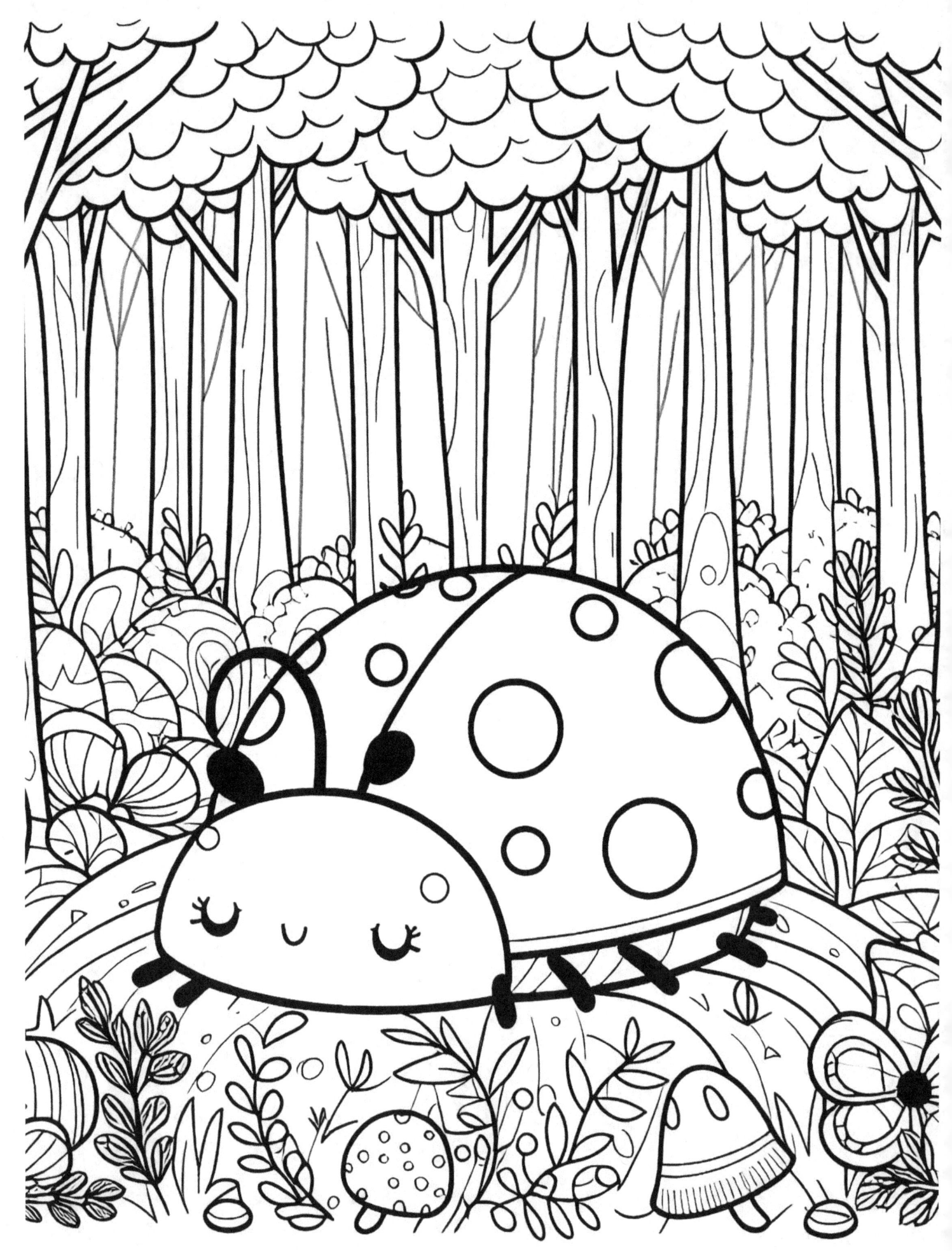

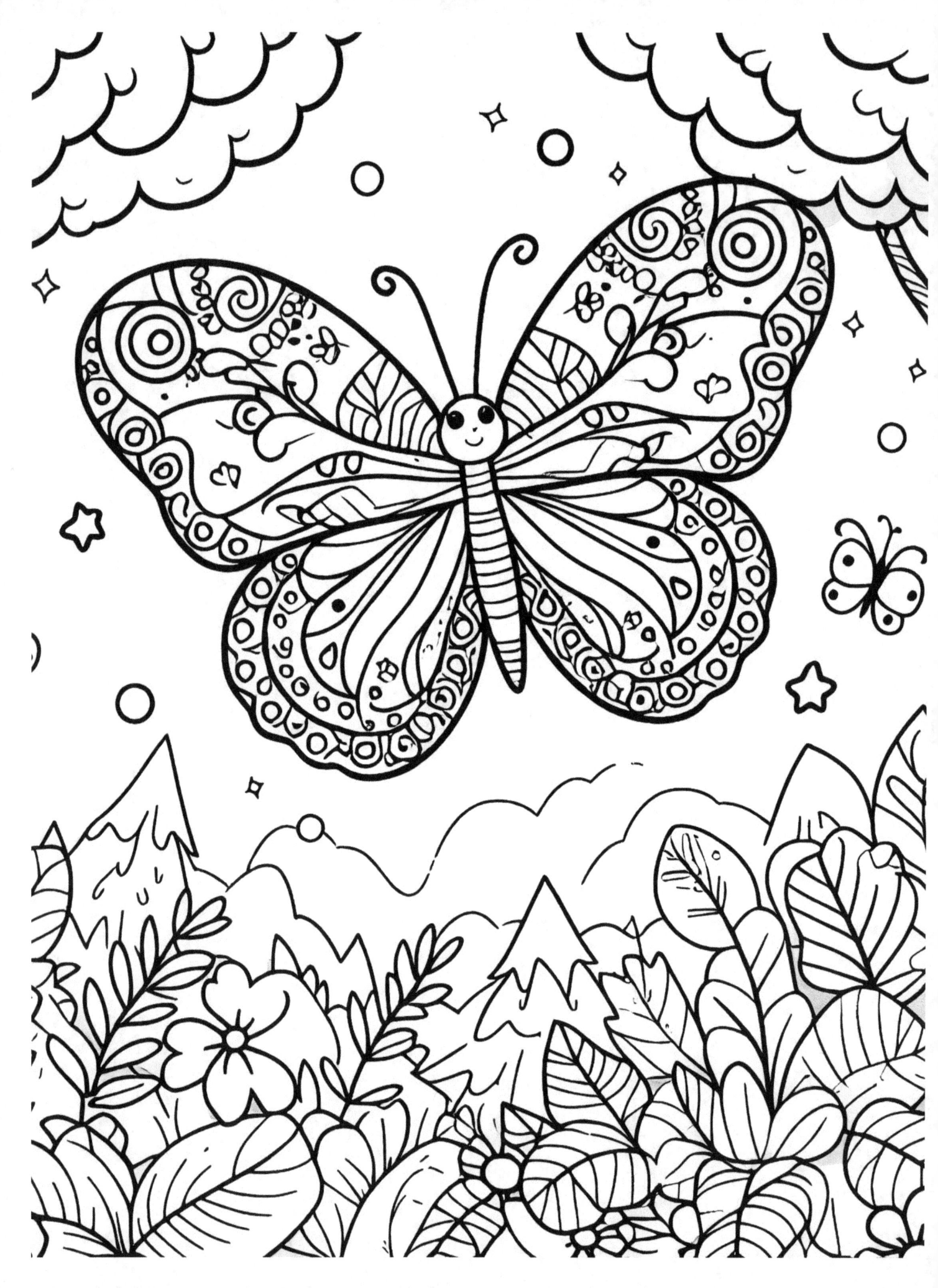

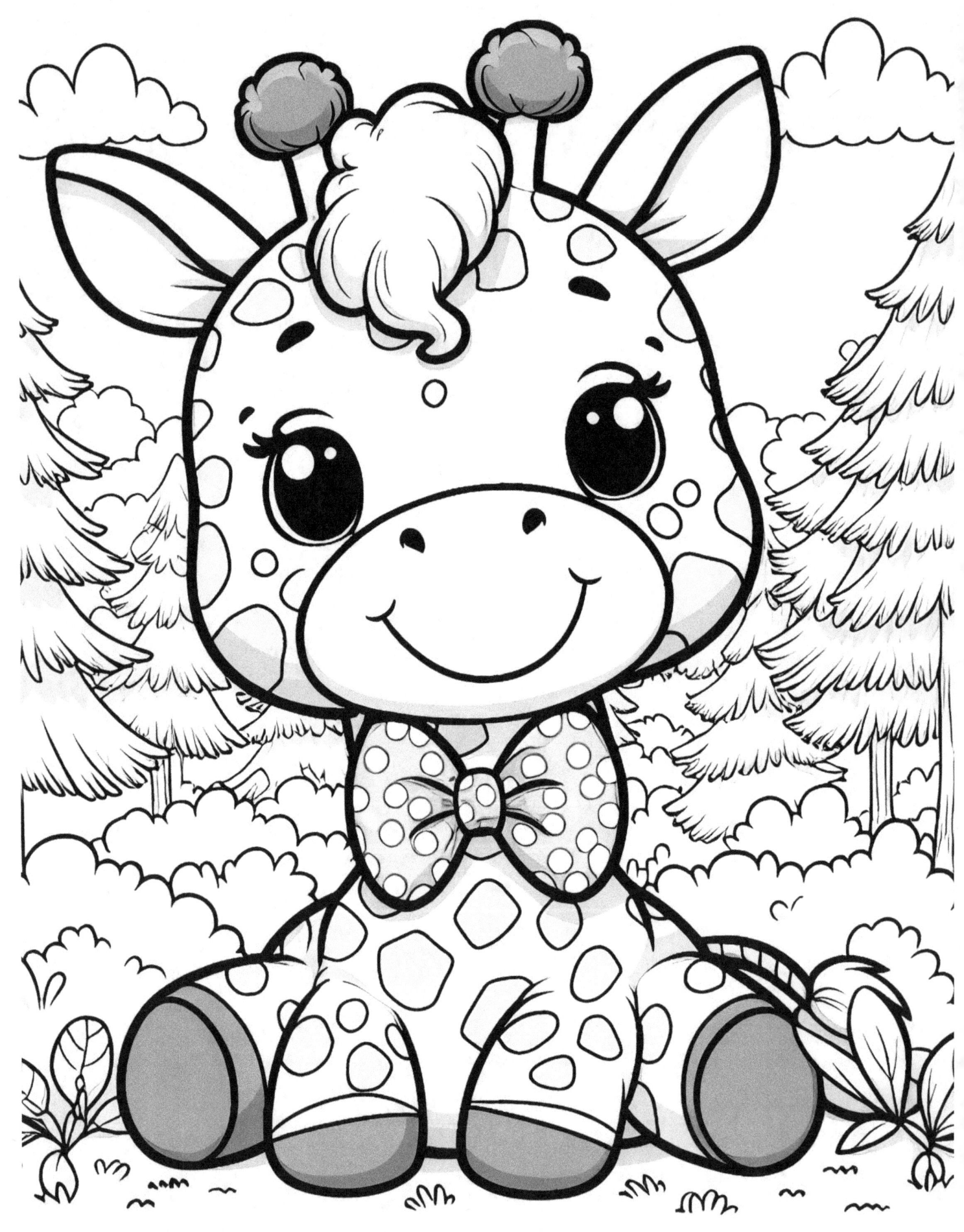

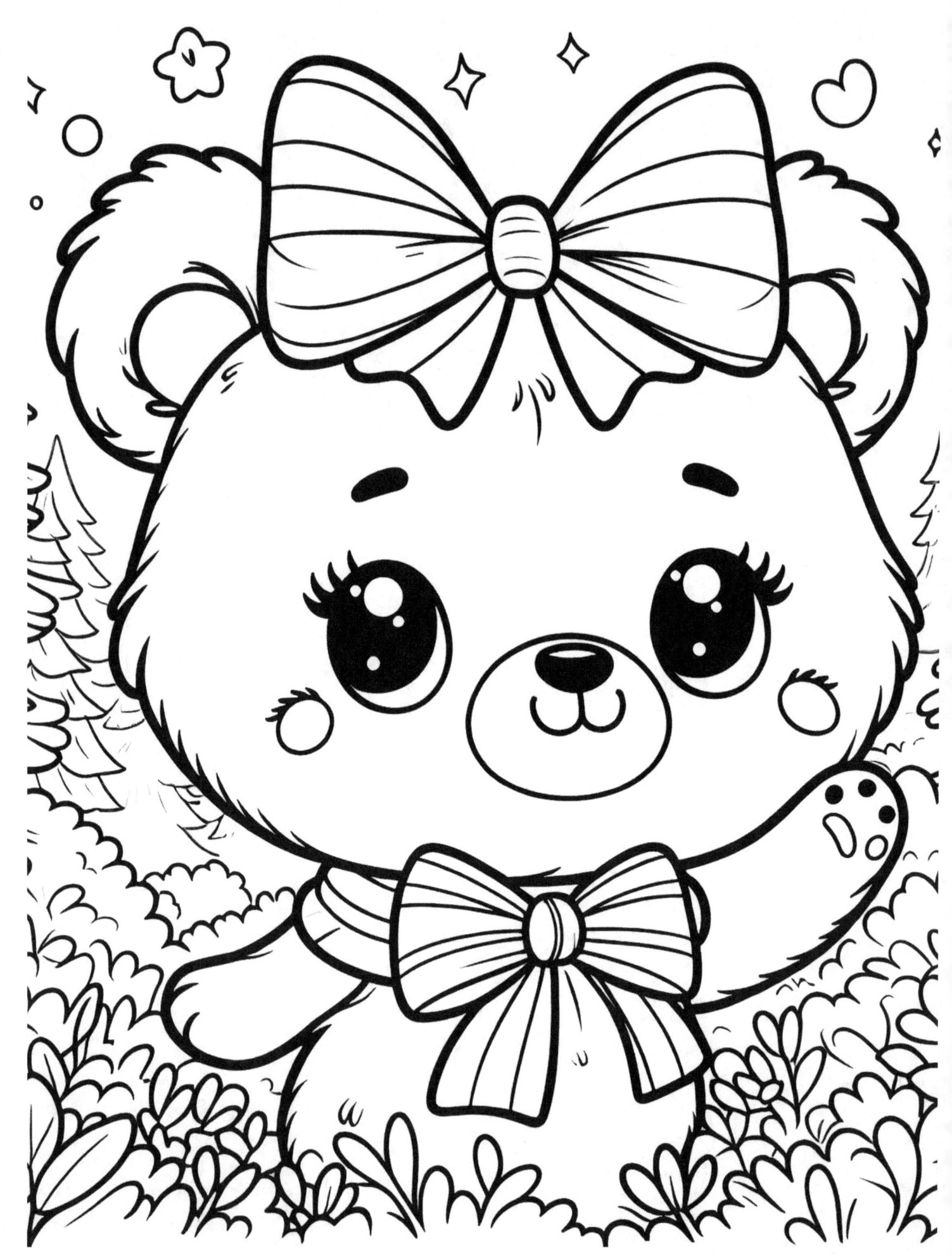

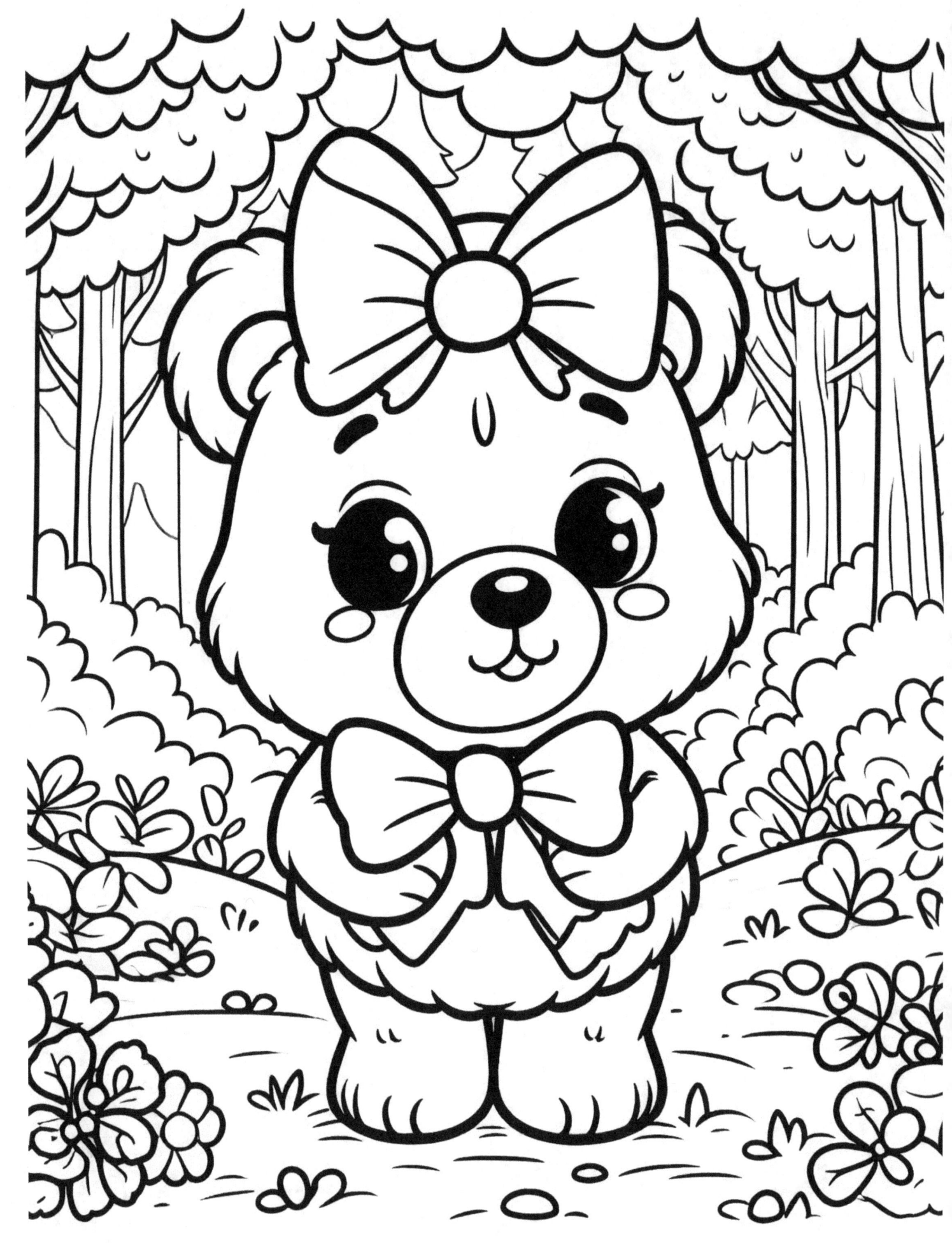

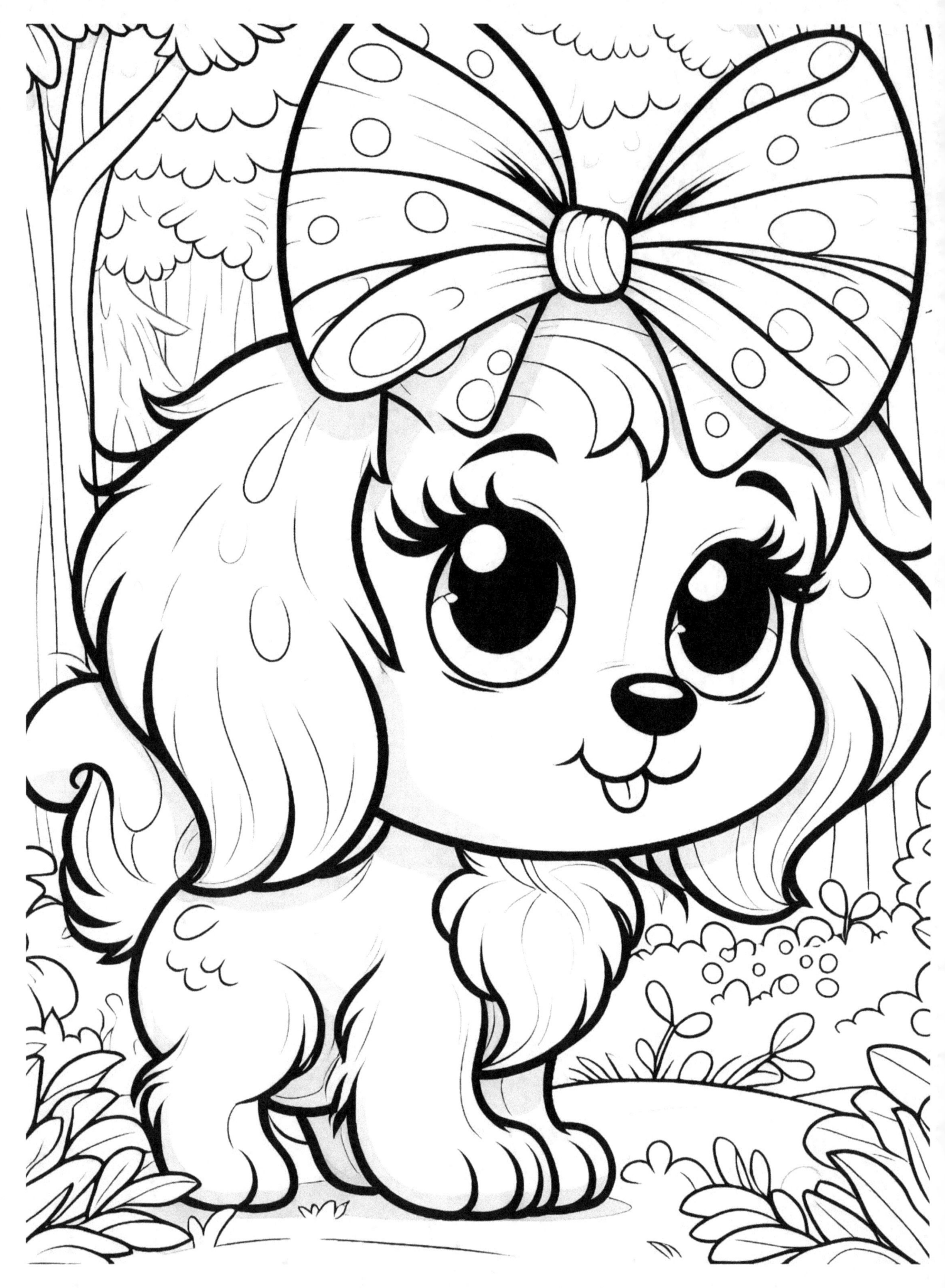

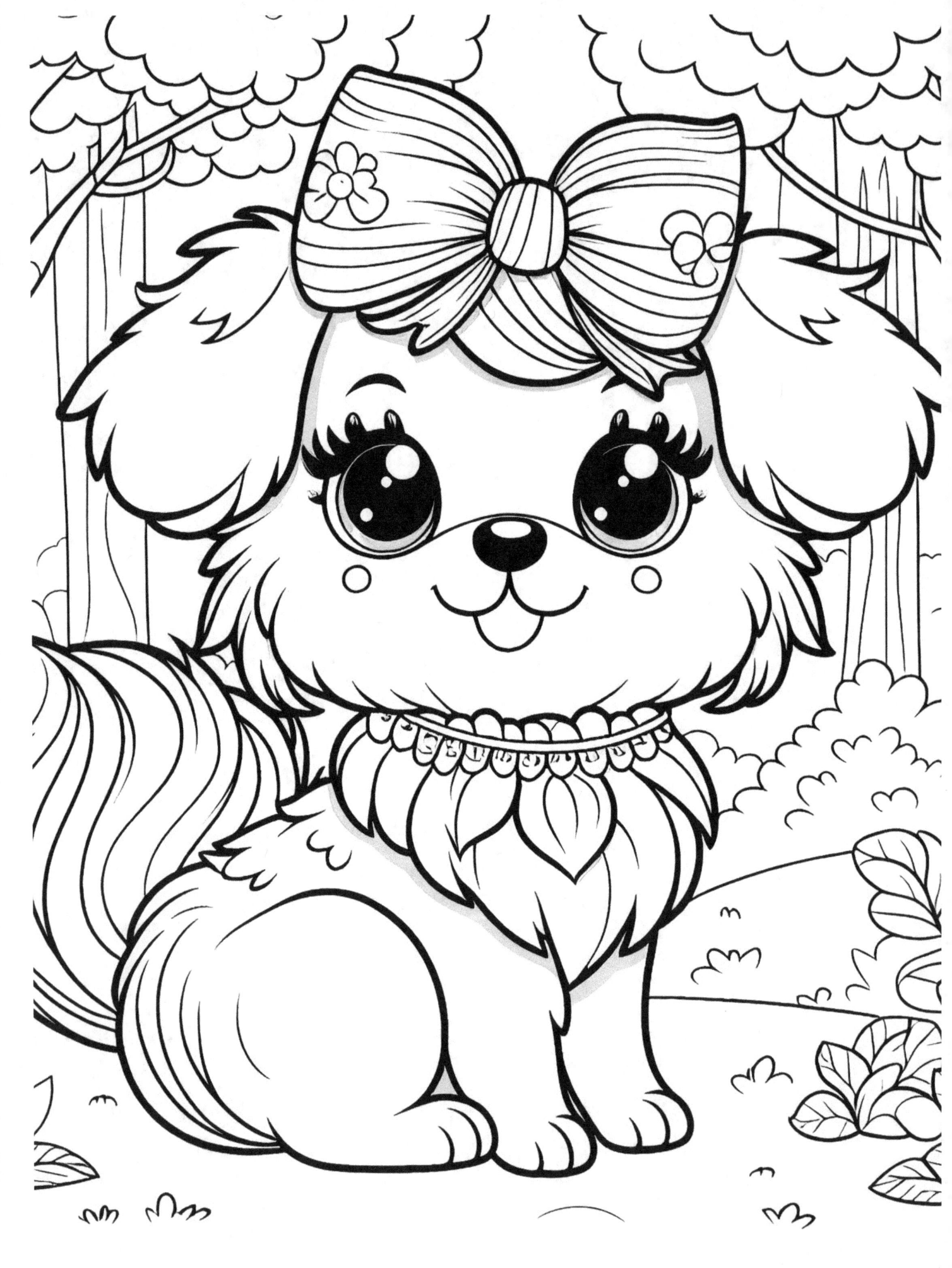

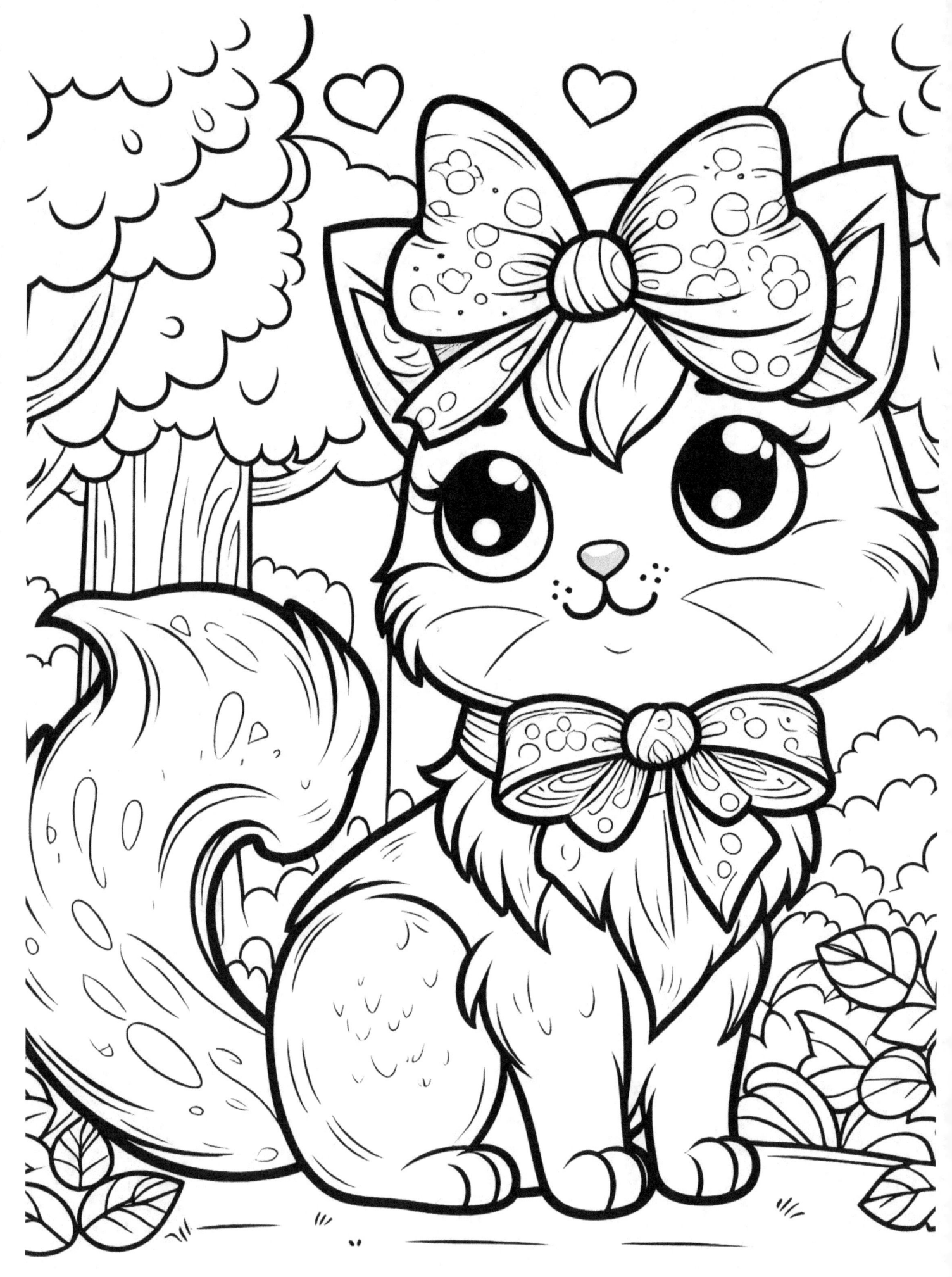

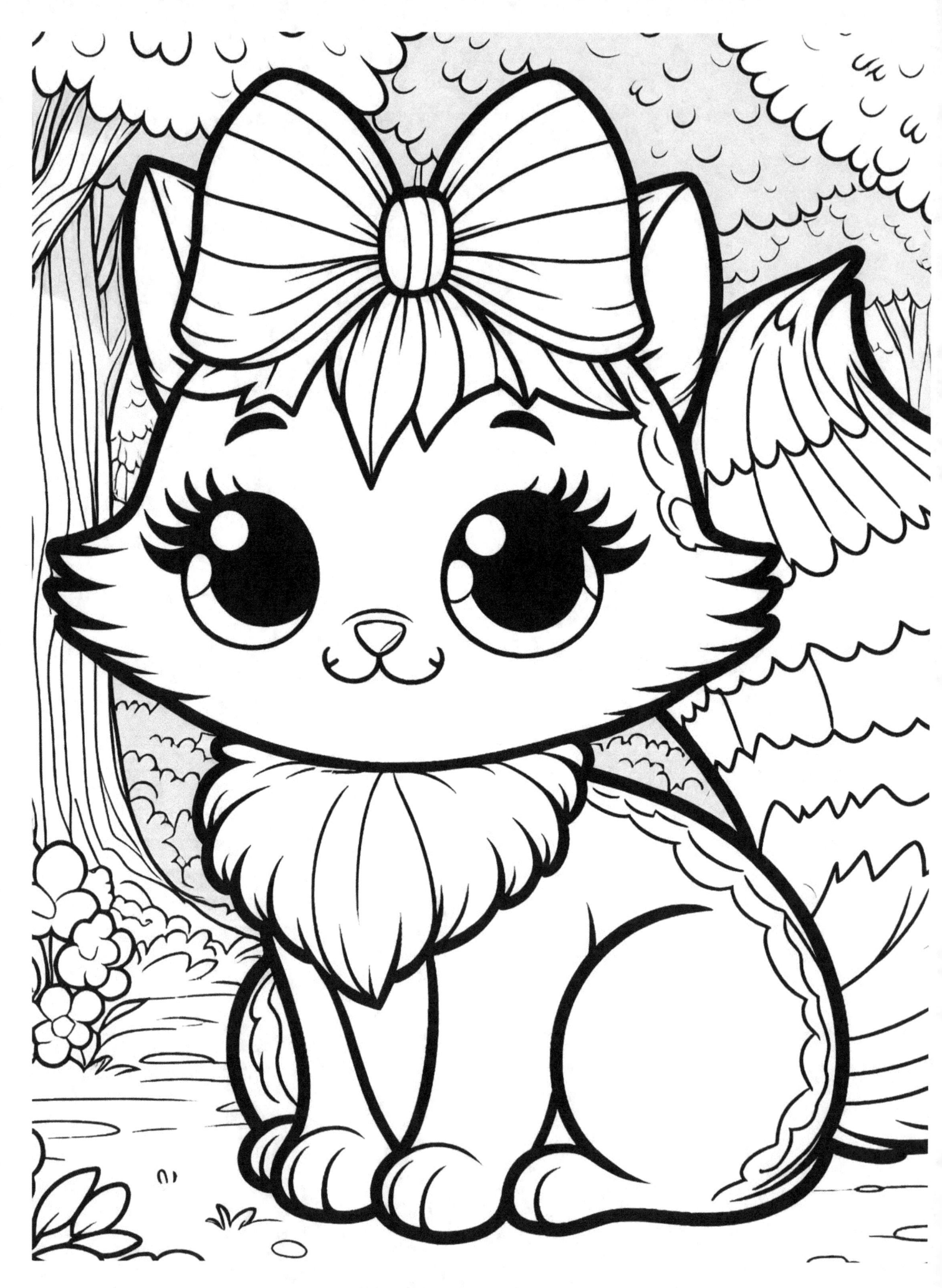

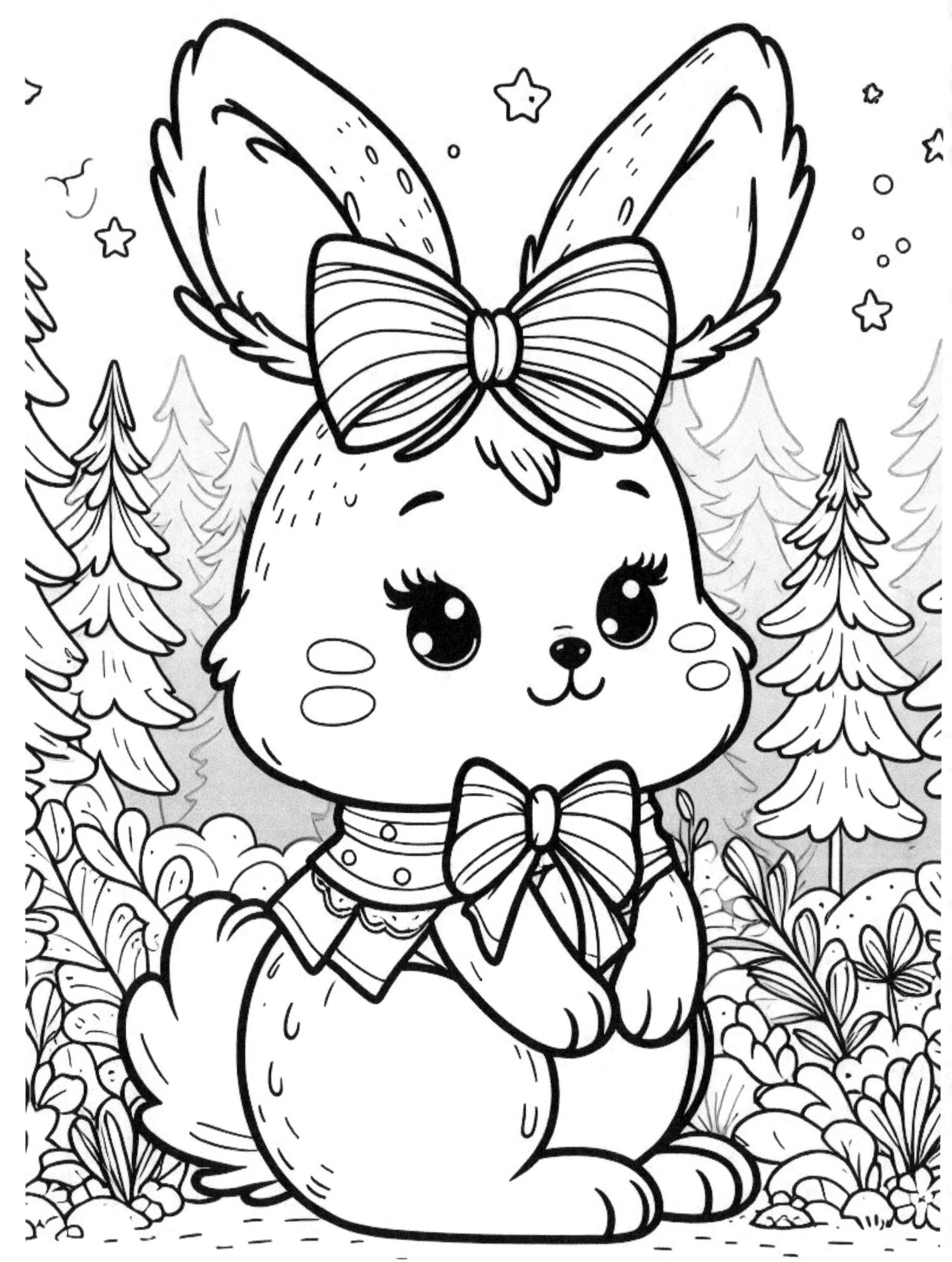

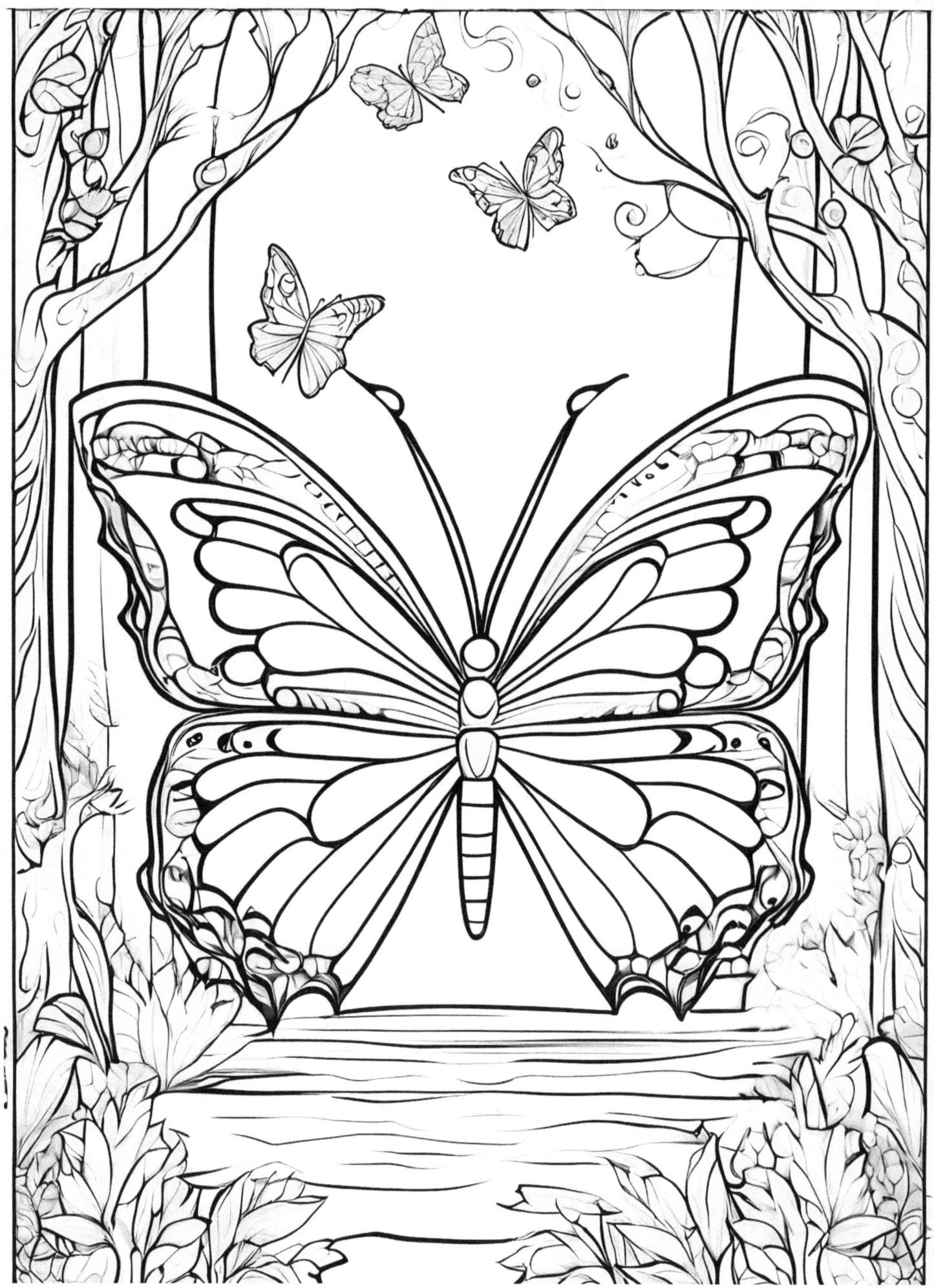

www.ingramcontent.com/pod-product-compliance
Lightning Source LLC
Chambersburg PA
CBHW062234220526
45471CB00009B/3482